Celebrating Differences

We All Look Different

by **Melissa Higgins**

raintree

a Capstone company — publishers for children

Raintree is an imprint of Capstone Global Library Limited, a company incorporated in England and Wales having its registered office at 264 Banbury Road, Oxford, OX2 7DY – Registered company number: 6695582

www.raintree.co.uk
myorders@raintree.co.uk

Text © Capstone Global Library Limited 2016
The moral rights of the proprietor have been asserted.

Jeni Wittrock, editor; Gene Bentdahl, designer; Svetlana Zhurkin, media researcher;
Kathy McColley, production specialist; Marcy Morin, studio scheduler; Sarah Schuette, photo stylist

ISBN 978 1 4747 2359 6
20 19 18 17 16
10 9 8 7 6 5 4 3 2 1

British Library Cataloguing in Publication Data
A full catalogue record for this book is available from the British Library.

Acknowledgements
We would like to thank the following for permission to reproduce photographs: Capstone Studio: Karon Dubke, cover; Dreamstime: James Blinn, 9; iStockphoto: Aldo Murillo, 20–21, Blend_Images, 7, Daniel Laflor, 5, Nina Shannon, 1; Photolibrary: Tim Jones, 19; Shutterstock: Distinctive Images, 15, GWImages, 17, Monkey Business Images, 10–11, Rob Hainer, 13.

We would like to thank Gail Saunders Smith, PhD and Donna Barkman, Children's Literature Specialist and Diversity Consultantant Ossining, New York for their invaluable help in the preparation of this book.

Every effort has been made to contact copyright holders of material reproduced in this book. Any omissions will be rectified in subsequent printings if notice is given to the publisher.

All the internet addresses (URLs) given in this book were valid at the time of going to press. However, due to the dynamic nature of the internet, some addresses may have changed, or sites may have changed or ceased to exist since publication. While the author and publisher regret any inconvenience this may cause readers, no responsibility for any such changes can be accepted by either the author or the publisher.

Note to parents and teachers

This book describes and illustrates differences in appearance. The images support early readers in understanding the text. The repetition of words and phrases helps early readers to learn new words. This book also introduces early readers to subject-specific vocabulary words, which are defined in the Glossary. Early readers may need assistance to read some words and to use the Contents, Glossary, Read more and Index sections of the book.

Made in China

Contents

I like the way I look

The way we look is one thing that makes you, *you* – and me, *me*. I like who I am. I like the things that make me unique.

We look different

Our skin is different colours.

My friends have cinnamon skin,

peach skin and chocolate skin.

We are all shapes and sizes.

Summer is our favourite time of year. The sun gives us more freckle power!

My hair is curly and yours
is straight. We both like going
to the library.

I am short and quick. I am
the fastest runner on my team.

We dress differently

The things I wear tell a story
about me. Orange is sunny
and happy, just like me.

My glasses help me to see.

Gran says my glasses

are picture frames for

my shining, brown eyes.

My leg braces help me get into
the game. I love to play
and work hard.

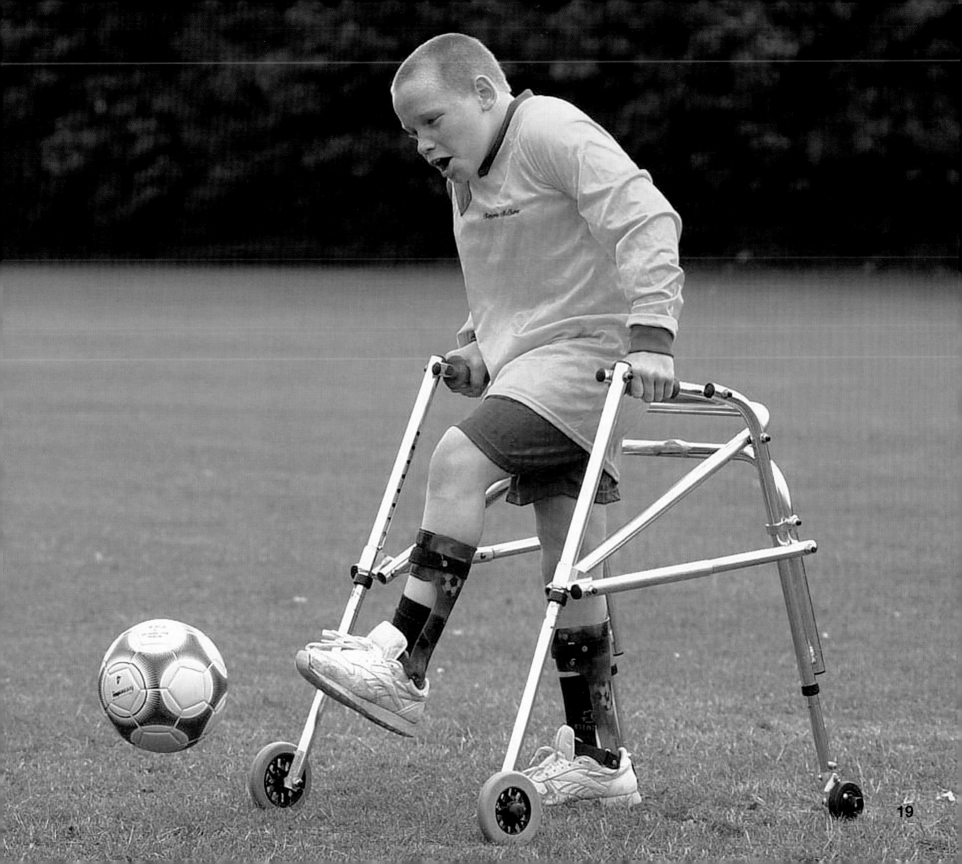

We like being different

Differences make life interesting. We are all one of a kind.

Glossary

brace frame worn around part of your body to support it

frame border that surrounds something, such as a picture frame

freckle small, light brown spot on a person's skin

unique one of a kind

Read more

I Know Someone with a Visual Impairment (Understanding Health Issues), Vic Parker (Raintree, 2012)

Millennium Children of Britain Just Like Me, Barnabas and Anabel Kindersley (Dorling Kindersley, 1999)

People of the World (Go Go Global), Nancy Loewen and Paula Skelley (Raintree, 2015)

Sammi and Dusty (City Farm), Jessie Williams (Curious Fox, 2013)

We Are All Different, Rebecca Rissman (Raintree, 2011)

What I Like About Me! A Book Celebrating Differences, Allia Zobel-Nolan (Reader's Digest Children's Books, 2005)

Index